OUP

The *Letter* to the *Colossians*

IN CHRIST ALONE

CWR

John Houghton

Copyright © 2006 CWR

Published 2006 by CWR, Waverley Abbey House, Waverley Lane, Farnham, Surrey GU9 8EP, UK. Registered Charity No. 294387. Registered Limited Company No. 1990308. Reprinted 2008, 2010, 2016, 2019.

The right of John Houghton to be identified as the author of this work has been asserted by him in accordance with the Copyright, Designs and Patents Act 1988, sections 77 and 78.

All rights reserved. No part of this publication may be reproduced, stored in a retrieval system, or transmitted, in any form or by any means, electronic, mechanical, photocopying, recording or otherwise, without the prior permission in writing of CWR.

For list of National Distributors, visit cwr.org.uk/distributors

Unless otherwise indicated, all Scripture references are from the Holy Bible: New International Version (NIV), copyright © 1973, 1978, 1984 by the International Bible Society.

Other version used:

NKJV: New King James Version, © 1982, Thomas Nelson Inc.

Concept development, editing, design and production by CWR

Cover image: Stock.xchng/Ben Lancaster

Printed in the UK by Linney.

ISBN: 978-1-85345-405-9

Contents

Introduction

The world of the Colossians was, spiritually speaking, surprisingly like ours. Roman peace, the Pax Romana, ensured a settled civilisation with a stable economy, good communications, adequate food supplies and little civil unrest. Yet good as these things were, the hearts of many people were dissatisfied. What had become of spiritual life? True, the official religion of Rome was in place and people dutifully paid lip service to the gods, but Rome was far away and few believed that political religion could ever satisfy the soul.

Instead, people were searching for deeper, more tangible roots to give their lives meaning. They turned to the ancient Greek and Roman mystery religions where it might be possible to enter a mystical state of being through ritual, self-denial and sacramental acts. By these means they sought to attain the beatific vision – a profound spiritual experience of the death and rebirth cycle that might grant them a form of afterlife. Today, in the nominally Christian West, we might equate this with the rise of the New Age movement and the interest in alternative spirituality.

It was into this world that a member of Paul's apostolic team, a man named Epaphras, came preaching the gospel. His mission field included the Lycus Valley in Asia Minor and it took him to the city of Colossae, where he had good success and founded a community of believers. Colossae itself had been a prosperous city noted for its glossy black wool, but in latter years was eclipsed by Laodicea and Hierapolis. However, it stood in a fertile valley on a main trade route from Ephesus to the East and as such retained an influence on the many traders who passed through – and with traders came ideas and religions.

Paul himself never visited the church in Colossae but received news of it from Epaphras. This led him to write to the church during his Roman imprisonment in AD 60. Delighted as he was by Epaphras's glowing report, Paul was also made aware of the encroachment of the mystery religions on the faith of these young converts. They faced two temptations. One was to combine their faith in Christ with elements from those other spiritualities – Eastern, Jewish, Greek and Roman mysticism. This is called 'syncretism'. It was later to flower into a full-blown threat to Christianity called 'Gnosticism'. The other was to feel that their faith came a poor second to these alternatives and their bold esoteric claims. This is called inferiority!

Paul tackles both, not by berating the Colossians, nor by condemning others' spiritual search out of hand. Instead, by encouragement and by using some of the same language and terminology as was used by the mystery religion adherents themselves, he demonstrates the adequacy, completeness and superiority of salvation in Christ alone.

Colossians is one of the most important New Testament books for us to study in today's climate of resurgent religious and spiritual interest. Historic Christendom may have had its day but there is a ready hearing for those who walk the earth with grace and humility, whose lives evidence an authentic spirituality demonstrated in wise living and love for our neighbours. For the challenge facing us today is not whether we will be spiritual – as opposed to merely religious – but what kind of spirituality will deliver the goods.

We hope that this study will help us understand better the hope within us and enable us more effectively to share our faith in Christ with those who are seeking to satisfy their spiritual hunger.

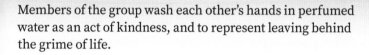

WEEK ONE

The Apostolic Heartbeat

Opening Icebreaker

Members of the group wash each other's hands in perfumed water as an act of kindness, and to represent leaving behind the grime of life.

Bible Readings

- Colossians 1:1–14
- Proverbs 8:1–7

Key Verse: 'For this reason, since the day we heard about you, we have not stopped praying for you and asking God to fill you with the knowledge of his will through all spiritual wisdom and understanding.' (1:9)

Focus: If you become a follower of the Way, you will qualify for a share in the world of spiritual enlightenment.

Opening Our Eyes

We in the West live under a remarkable materialistic peace, but it has not satisfied our souls. Many people are searching for something better; they are engaging in a spiritual journey to find the inner wholeness that no amount of retail therapy or overseas travel can deliver. At the same time, the majority of the population has dismissed historic Christianity as violent, chauvinistic and irrelevant. Today's searchers are drawn more to paganism – to the earth-mother mysticism of Gaia, or Isis, or the Sacred Prostitute – in their quest for enlightenment.

But supposing there is another route to wholeness: a set of secret mysteries discovered by a community dwelling in the Lycus Valley – citizens of ancient Colossae who called themselves followers of the Way. What had they found, and could it transform our lives today?

We learn about this community from a letter written by one of the leading teachers of the Way, Paul of Tarsus. He addresses his readers as *holy ones* – people set apart – and he starts by commending them for their lifestyle of faith, hope and practical love. The teaching they had received was in fact not unique to them, but was spreading like a fruitful plant all over the known world. However, it was not imposed by imperial might or religious dictatorship; this was a grass-roots movement spread by humble messengers like Epaphras.

Paul and Timothy were delighted to receive Epaphras's report concerning this new group of followers and it had stimulated them to pray for their spiritual development ever since. Specifically, they prayed for them to experience a full revelation of the mind of God. This is no mere intellectual quest, but is a different kind of intelligence – genuine spiritual wisdom. Not that this should make them proud or self-gratifying. Rather it is so that they might live transformed, God-pleasing lives in their community. Nor is this a pathway of sombre religion or flesh-denying asceticism. Their growing spiritual enlightenment will fill them with joy and thanksgiving, so that they might persevere in their new-found faith, whatever the difficulties.

Paul reminds them that their discovery of the Way has qualified them for a glorious future, an inheritance that is no less than eternal life – the birthright of all those set apart for the kingdom of light. These Colossians and their fellow believers have been liberated from the prison house of spiritual tyranny and darkness. Now they have a new citizenship in the realm of light. It is not a hard-earned right but a free gift from the Divine Source Himself – God the Father. Yet it is not cheap; the Father's filial expression, the Son, paid a high price for their spiritual salvation. For at the root of their questing and ours lies the insurmountable problem of personal evil and corruption. We need more than enlightenment; we need redemption. God's Son offered up His own life so that all followers of the Way might experience the forgiveness of sins.

Faith in the Son of God that is demonstrated in transformed behaviour is the surest proof of genuine spiritual experience. This is why Paul describes the Colossians as 'holy and faithful brothers' and offers the benediction of grace and peace upon their lives. Such primitive purity challenges our own faith and its outworking. Do we find ourselves sharing the same apostolic heartbeat as these Colossians? Or have we settled for less?

Discussion Starters

1. How do you view New Age seekers? Are they demonised to the eyeballs, or have they something to add to our faith? Or are they on the road towards Christ and just need our help?

2. What is the difference between Bible knowledge and spiritual wisdom?

3. If true spiritual wisdom is demonstrated by our lifestyle, what practical characteristics should that lifestyle incorporate?

4. We need more than enlightenment; we need redemption. Discuss.

5. Describe how you make the journey from the kingdom of darkness to the kingdom of light.

_____

_____

_____

_____

6. How would you describe and explain 'the inheritance of the saints' to a spiritual seeker?

_____

_____

_____

_____

7. Paul's missionary vision stirred him to pray. What kind of missionary vision do you have and how do you respond to it?

_____

_____

_____

_____

Personal Application

Christian is as Christian does. Few are impressed by mere intellectual proofs of the faith; not many are touched by charismatic demonstrations of power. The presence of Christ in our lives that reveals us to be people of grace and peace is the most powerful testimony we can bear. Followers of the Way must also show the way by the quality of their lives.

We do so especially by the quality of our relationships, both within the believing community and in the world at large. The gospel is still spreading like a fruitful vine; let us examine our lives to ensure that we are not dead wood but are 'bearing fruit in every good work'.

Seeing Jesus in the Scriptures

Are your sins forgiven? It's a simple question but of vital importance. We are held captive in the kingdom of darkness by a blindness induced by 'the god of this age' (2 Cor. 4:4), but that darkness is more than ignorance. It is moral. We are dead in trespasses and sins and held captive by our guilty conscience.

There is One who was born free of corruption. His name is Jesus and He is the Son of God. Coming from the realm of light, He is uniquely qualified to help us. Sacrificing His life on our behalf, Jesus bore the guilt that is ours; He paid the ultimate price for our forgiveness and redemption. In doing so, He disarmed the accusatory and controlling powers and authorities, making it possible for us to be released into the kingdom of light.

WEEK TWO

Firstborn Glory

Opening Icebreaker

Go around the group and ask, 'What is the best thing you have ever made and how much of yourself did you put into it (eg models, cakes, events, etc)?'

Bible Readings

- Colossians 1:15–23
- Philippians 2:5–11
- Proverbs 8:22–31
- 2 Corinthians 5:16–20

Key Verse: 'For God was pleased to have all his fulness dwell in him'. (1:19)

Focus: Our faith reconnects us to the source of all life and existence.

Opening Our Eyes

Who is this anointed Expression of the Divine Source, this Son of the Father? He is the *ikon* of God. An 'icon', in its classic religious use and in modern computer usage, is a representation and a doorway. The Son fulfils both functions for us. He shows us what God is like and He is the way for us to encounter the Father. Click on Him and you enter the world of spiritual reality.

That reality takes us back to the dawn of creation where the Son – the Firstborn in status and the ultimate expression of God's wisdom – is revealed to be the construction engineer and custodian of the whole created order. He is also the divine glue, the cosmological binding force that holds together the entire spiritual world and the structure of matter itself – what some call 'the fire in the equations'. Without the Son, the universe would simply collapse and cease to exist.

The only way to understand God is to see God interpreted by God for our own eyes – and that is what the Son does. Not only do we see the power of God but also the vulnerability intrinsic to His love. For the Son took on real humanity; He lived among us, identifying fully with our frailty and mortality.

This is an astonishing revelation, but all the more so when we discover that the Son became willingly the murder victim of an unholy alliance between fundamentalist religion and political imperialism. Crucified by timeservers, the Life dies! Yet He does so on our behalf, reaching out to our alienation with nail-pierced hands and calling us to be reconciled to a God from whom we have distanced ourselves by our bad behaviour.

This is just the beginning of the story. God raises His Son from the dead. What is modelled in the physical cycle of nature is true also of the spiritual. Yet it is no ghost that rises. The divine glue is no alien to the material world. He is fully, physically, raised from the dead to be the Head, not of disembodied spirits, but of a new creation. The Lord of the first creation is now the Lord of the second. God has invested in Him His own essence and commissioned Him to bring about a cosmic reconciliation that will bring universal peace. Through His shed blood He will abolish all the disharmony, corruption and injustice in the universe.

Where will He start? With His enemies; with those of us who did not love Him and whose behaviour was an offence to His purity. We can be reconciled to God and to each other and become members of that stream of renewed humanity that calls itself Christ's Body.

We do not need a lengthy self-help programme to achieve this. It is instead a committed act of faith that we choose to maintain in the hope that we – now spiritually made alive – will one day experience a physical rebirth that will abolish mortality. Eternal life, no less!

A new force is at work in the world. The Number One of the first creation has been appointed the Number One of an emerging new creation. By identifying ourselves with Him and acknowledging His lordship over our lives, we take our place in the vanguard of the future – 2 Corinthians 5:17. It is good news indeed, and a message to be shared with the whole of creation!

Discussion Starters

1. How much of a divide should there be between science
    and faith, given that the material and the spiritual
    universe owe their direct origin and maintenance
    to the Son?

    _____
    _____
    _____
    _____

2. If the Son is the Head of the Church, what are the
    practical implications for us in our weekly church life?

    _____
    _____
    _____
    _____

3. Many talk about Gaia today, encouraging worship and
    respect for the planet and endowing it with female
    personality. Since the Son made 'Mother Nature', how
    would you address a modern-day nature worshipper?

    _____
    _____
    _____
    _____

4. The fullness, the wholeness, the harmony, the 'Wow!' of
    God dwells in the Son. What do you think this means?

    _____
    _____
    _____
    _____

5. 'Shalom' is the Hebrew word for peace, well-being and wholeness. In an age when many are seeking shalom through a variety of techniques and experiences, what can you offer?

_____

_____

_____

_____

6. Calling us 'enemies' of God seems rather strong. Why do you think Paul used this term?

_____

_____

_____

_____

7. How can we help one another continue in the faith without wavering?

_____

_____

_____

_____

Personal Application

What we call 'Church' should be defined not by ecclesiastical structures and traditions but by its relationship to the Head. It is the physical manifestation of our risen Lord Jesus Christ Himself. What people see and encounter through us is what they know of Christ. This high and holy calling to be His honoured representatives requires a stability of faith. Plenty will challenge and test us. Some will seek to lead us astray, enticing us to mix the truth with error in the name of tolerance. They will say our faith is redundant. Do not heed them. We have connected to the Source of all life and existence and the future beckons us. Who needs anything less?

Seeing Jesus in the Scriptures

When followers of Christ call Him 'Lord', they are proclaiming the good news of a new government that operates not from an earthly capital but from heaven itself. The good news has been proclaimed to all creatures under heaven. Imagine a palace making a public proclamation of a new ruler. The announcement is published on the palace gates. The job of the messengers is then to ensure that everyone gets to hear the news.

We have heard that God has appointed Jesus as the Lord of all, and one day, in despair or in adoration, every knee will bow to Him. Meanwhile, He is exercising a mission of reconciliation through us – 'We implore you on Christ's behalf: Be reconciled to God' (2 Cor. 5:20). Do you have peace with God, and have you now become one of His ambassadors of peace?

WEEK THREE

The Mystery Uncovered

Opening Icebreaker

Play 'Pass-the-Parcel' (see Leader's Notes).

Bible Readings

* Colossians 1:24–2:3
* Romans 8:5–11

Key Verse: 'To them God has chosen to make known among the Gentiles the glorious riches of this mystery, which is Christ in you, the hope of glory.' (1:27)

Focus: We labour to bring to birth the revelation of Christ.

Opening Our Eyes

Human autonomy is a myth. We humans are spirit-dependent creatures. We are all possessed of some spirit or other: it just depends on which and to what extent. Disciples of the Way do not merely follow a set of doctrines or behaviour codes. The Spirit of Christ Himself dwells within them and motivates them to serve His cause. Indeed, if anyone does not have the Spirit of Christ, they do not belong to Christ.

'Enchristing' – Christ in us – is the central mystery of true faith and one that is only truly revealed to those devoted to Christ – which is why our critics betray such abysmal ignorance of our faith. Christ in us is the most profound and wonderful form of spirit possession. There is nothing evil or manipulative in this; Christ comes by invitation only, and He does so to grant us intimate fellowship with the God of love. His personal indwelling is the essence of spiritual life and the guarantee of our bodily resurrection and of eternal life – the hope of glory.

But who is this Christ? The Greek term translates the Hebrew expectation of a Messiah and means 'the Anointed', a term we will use interchangeably to keep its meaning before us. This mysterious figure emerges from the Old Testament in such a manner as to confuse all but the spiritually discerning. He really is a secret – a mystery revealed only to seekers of sufficient integrity, dedication and humility. Yet this much is clear: He will be filled with the Spirit of God like no one else. He will be a suffering Servant, offering Himself for the ills and evils of others. He will set people free from political, spiritual, economic and personal oppression. He will rule all the nations of the world in righteousness, justice and mercy.

Commonly, the Jewish people understood this in nationalistic terms, which is why many of them struggled when the fulfilment of the prophecies turned up in person. Jesus of Nazareth did not fit a nationalistic mindset and He refused to play along. And the Gentiles would never have heard of Him at all were it not for the work of the apostles – in particular, the labours of the apostle Paul.

Having encountered the risen Jesus on the Damascus road, Paul became a passionate, tireless and devoted ambassador of this mystery. His commission focused especially on proclaiming the good news to the Gentile world. Jesus' sufferings became his as he struggled to handle the immense evangelistic and apostolic energy of the Anointed within him, longing for his hearers to be robust in faith and united in love. For then they would enter the depths of this mystery; they would cross the spiritual threshold and discover the thesaurus of wisdom and knowledge hidden within Him. In short, to know the Anointed, to be in Him, and to have Him possess our beings, is to uncover the key to everything. He is the Holy Grail; He is the philosopher's stone; He is the meaning of life.

Little wonder then that the apostle felt so committed to the task. His zeal challenges our laid-back, pew-warming complacency. Apostolic tradition has to do with much more than what we believe; it is concerned with how we believe. To be possessed of the Spirit of the Anointed, to be custodians of the profoundest truth, to be heirs with Him of eternal life, must surely compel us to tell the whole world of our discovery.

Discussion Starters

1. What do you think characterises those in whom the Spirit of Christ (the Anointed) dwells?

   _____

   _____

   _____

   _____

2. People seek all sorts of 'possession' today. What reasons can you give as to why someone should wish to be possessed by the Spirit of Christ?

   _____

   _____

   _____

   _____

3. 'Christianity is all about doing good works to get a place in heaven.' How do you wish to respond to this statement?

   _____

   _____

   _____

   _____

4. What do you think Paul meant when he claimed to 'fill up in [his] flesh what is still lacking in regard to Christ's afflictions'?

   _____

   _____

   _____

   _____

5. In what ways do you consider the Church continues in Christ's sufferings today?

_____

_____

_____

_____

6. What clues does Paul give us in our quest for a deeper appreciation of the mystery of Christ?

_____

_____

_____

_____

7. How might we re-energise ourselves for the task of bringing this message of salvation to our world?

_____

_____

_____

_____

Personal Application

It is easy for those raised within the fold of the Church to take the mystery of Christ for granted. Those increasing numbers who come from outside view it differently. Discovering Christ in His fullness is to them simply awesome! In days when so much of our faith has focused on Church, growth, repackaging and marketing, when our life is measured by our social activism, we do well to remember the spiritual heart of our message. For if we take for granted or lose the mystery of Christ within us, we have nothing of lasting worth or spiritual importance to offer a needy world. Our doing must flow from our being, and not the other way round.

Seeing Jesus in the Scriptures

The sufferings of Christ are not yet over. Although He has done everything necessary to secure our eternal redemption on the cross, is raised from the dead and is now seated at the Father's right hand, the completion of His work awaits its finale. The King of kings continues to endure humiliation on earth. Dwelling in His people by His Spirit, He bears insult, spite, persecution and hatred as He works to reconcile the world though our instrumentality. His sufferings overflow into our own lives. Paul felt it in his own flesh, and so do we. Co-heirs with Christ we may be, but we must 'share in his sufferings in order that we may also share in his glory' (Rom. 8:17). That is why we continue to pray, 'Your kingdom come'.

WEEK FOUR

True and False Spirituality

Opening Icebreaker

Play a game of inventing a new religion. What ideas and practices would you include to make this work as a viable religion?

Bible Readings

- Colossians 2:4–23
- Romans 6:1–11
- 1 Timothy 4:1–5

Key Verse: 'See to it that no-one takes you captive through hollow and deceptive philosophy, which depends on human tradition and the basic principles of this world rather than on Christ.'(2:8)

Focus: Spiritual technology will not change the heart.

Opening Our Eyes

Vanity is an ever-present challenge to pure, unsophisticated faith in Christ. It takes many forms, and all of them are a distraction from the importance of putting down nourishing roots into Christ that are able to sustain real spiritual growth and fruitfulness.

False ideologies based on Western secular humanism, Eastern mysticism or legalistic Judaism all share a common paradigm – the basic principles of this world. The apostle John sums these up as: 'the lust of the flesh, the lust of the eyes, and the pride of life' (1 John 2:16, NKJV). These philosophies are predatory. They sound sophisticated, particularly in their 'pick 'n' mix' form, but given the chance, they will rob you of your faith.

The vaunted claims of worldly vanity do not compare with the qualities of the Anointed. Risen from the dead and possessing a supra-physical resurrection body, He encapsulates the fullness of God's virtues and His eternal essence. He is the supreme authority above all other gurus, experts, politicians and prophets and His followers are privileged to share that same fullness of spiritual life.

Built into creation is the paradigm of life, death and rebirth. It is one of the fundamental truths about God and lies at the heart of Jesus' teaching. Indeed, so prevalent is this paradigm that conversion, initiation and rebirthing ceremonies are universal, even among atheists. In other philosophies the old life is often characterised by ignorance. However, it is also morally decadent; we are 'dead' in our sins of disobedience to God's will. We carry within us a nature predisposed to wrongdoing.

Rebirthing (or 'new birth') for followers of the Way takes place when we enter into spiritual union and identify ourselves with Christ. His circumcision (representing the cutting off of the sinful nature) and His baptism (representing His death on the cross and His burial), and His resurrection (representing renewed life) become ours. The transforming power of this spiritual union with Christ is awesome; it sets us free from slavery to sin and to the sinful nature, and gifts us with genuine divine life – Romans 6:6–8.

Furthermore, Jesus took our contract of slavery with all its rules and regulations and crucified it. He rendered it null and void. Our former slave masters, the spiritual authorities and powers that undergird the basic principles of the world, have been publicly disempowered. Grace has triumphed over law, freedom over slavery. The point of Jesus' greatest weakness was also the point of greatest triumph.

You are free and complete in the Anointed. Don't be drawn back into the shadowlands of religious legalism where you are judged by your diet and ritual observances. Avoid pious superstition that will make more fuss over visions of saints and angels than it will over Christ Himself. We should not be impressed by those who make much of their supposed spiritual insights. Rather than a mark of spiritual advancement they are in reality a sign of disconnection from the true Head who nurtures the organic life of the Body of Christ.

You died to these worldly paradigms, so why act as though you were still subject to them? People love making up rules that are supposed to better us. But that's all they are – human rules, and they don't work. You can try mantras, diets, rituals, self-mutilation, ceremonies, trances, self-denial, pilgrimages – whatever – but they won't make a scrap of difference to your inner person and its selfish cravings. Real wisdom for living lies elsewhere.

Discussion Starters

1. Why do you think people are so obsessed with self-help programmes today? Why don't they work?

2. How do you answer someone who recommends a rebirthing experience for you?

3. In what ways can we find ourselves guilty of adding rules and regulations to our faith in Christ?

4. Explore what it means to be in union with Christ, especially in His death, burial and resurrection.

5. What forms do 'hollow and deceptive philosophies' most commonly take today? How do you deal with them?

_____

_____

_____

_____

6. How can we ensure that we do not add, subtract or deviate from the purity and completeness of our faith in Christ alone?

_____

_____

_____

_____

7. Why do you think Paul uses such strong language when he instructs Timothy about the spirit of the age in 1 Timothy 4:1–5?

_____

_____

_____

_____

Personal Application

We live in an increasingly religious age and our media is full of ideas for self-improvement, inner wholeness and better relationships. While we do not despise the desire for such things, we find the answer in our union with Christ. Sadly, many of us have yet to appropriate the full reality of this. Too often our lives appear as screwed up and frustrated as those of our neighbours. Inner peace and grace are sometimes lacking in our demeanour and all people see is our religious observance. Little wonder that so many prefer to describe themselves as 'spiritual rather than religious', and 'believing without belonging'.

Let us ensure that we are living in the resurrection light of the Anointed and not merely in the shadowlands of religious profession.

Seeing Jesus in the Scriptures

The heart of the Christian faith is Christ Himself. No saint or angel, no prophet or religious teacher, no miracle worker or evangelist comes near Him. In Christ alone is found the complete nature of God. You want to know what God is like? Then meet Jesus!

The Anointed is the Head, the One above all others. Whatever claims are made for other religious leaders, whatever forces of darkness and light there may be, whatever political organisations, leaders and power bases there are, Christ is supreme over all of them. Jesus Christ is Lord of all, and this by the decree of God the Father Himself. Let us never settle for less, let alone try to take any glory to ourselves.

WEEK FIVE

Old Man, New Man

Opening Icebreaker

Imagine you have emigrated and taken on the citizenship of a new country. What would you need to do to become fully naturalised? How might your behaviour change?

Bible Readings

- Colossians 3:1–16
- Romans 5:17–19

Key Verse: 'For you died, and your life is now hidden with Christ in God.' (3:3)

Focus: True spirituality transforms our heart attitudes.

Opening Our Eyes

There is only one man who has the right to be in heaven and His name is Jesus the Anointed. None of us can inherit eternal life in our own name. We are either in Him, sharing His name and nature and living in His anointing, or we are in Adam, sharing his name and nature and living under judgment and death. Christ is seated at God's right hand; He holds the position of highest honour and authority and those who share His name and nature have been raised to the same status. This being so, we should focus our attention heavenwards rather than be indulging in the corrupting influences of the world.

Implicit in our experience of spiritual rebirth is a death to the death-dealing qualities of Adam and a resurrection to the life-giving qualities of Christ. Here is the heart of the mystery: your life is encrypted in God, and Christ is the unbreakable algorithm that secures your eternal salvation. No spiritual hacker, not even the devil himself, could ever hope to crack Him and steal your inheritance. You may not look much like an heir to eternal life, but you are, and at Christ's return you will appear with Him in glory for all to see.

This will profoundly affect our outlook and behaviour. We will want to nurture our heavenly future rather than dwell in our earthbound past. True spirituality has a genuinely moral dimension; it affects our attitudes, our perspective and our conduct among our relatives, friends, neighbours and colleagues. The contrast will often appear quite stark. Paul lists some of the typical attitudes of 'earth-ism': sexual immorality, impurity, lusts, evil desires, idolatrous greed.

It is these attitudes and behaviour patterns that earn the displeasure of God and demand justice to be done for our wilful moral abuse of God's created order. Ditch them, along with all the offensive speech defects of the world. They no longer belong to you because you have undergone an identity change; you have stripped off your former self and put on your new self. You are learning to be a true human being all over again. No longer are you defined by your race or religion – or your educational and economic condition and background, or your cultural and social tradition. Instead, you are defined by Christ. You are in the process of being remade in the image of God, no less!

As God's loved and chosen race we will want to be characterised by the virtues of Christ: compassion, kindness, humility, gentleness and patience. Forgiveness, acceptance and toleration of one another's frailties will become our instinct. After all, the Lord has forgiven us, hasn't He? Our forgiveness must become as unconditional as His.

Embracing all these virtues and tying them together to perfection is love itself. Spiritual maturity is not some arid perfectionism that owes more to stoical self-discipline and social advantage than it does to the grace of Christ. The truly mature (perfect in the sense of 'fully grown') are those who love others with the sacrificial love of Christ.

The authentic Church is God's Peace Corps. In the body of the Anointed we cease our worldly striving and experience the peace of Christ. It is a context for thanksgiving where Christ's Word matters more than ours. It is the place for spiritual enrichment where we can sing the songs of grace that teach and correct one another and give expression to our gratitude to the Lord.

Discussion Starters

1. What do you think it will be like to appear with Christ in glory? When will it happen?

_____

_____

_____

_____

2. It is sometimes disparagingly noted that someone is so heavenly minded that they are of no earthly use. Unfortunately, most of us are so earthly minded that we are of no heavenly use. Discuss.

_____

_____

_____

_____

3. Tribalism, be it ethnic, cultural or religious, causes more conflict than just about anything else on earth. If Christ abolishes these divisions, how can we apply the gospel in situations of conflict and minister His peace?

_____

_____

_____

_____

4. Forgiveness is fundamental to the Christian faith. Should we only forgive when people ask for pardon, or should we forgive anyway? Does 'forgiveness' imply that we are condoning evil actions by letting people off lightly?

_____

_____

_____

_____

5. How much do you think it is worth making a distinction between 'psalms, hymns and spiritual songs'? Why is division over musical preferences so prevalent both in the world and in the Church?

6. How can we improve the ways that we 'teach and admonish one another with all wisdom'? Is this just more sermons and Bible studies or is it something more?

7. How can we best communicate to those around us that the secret of the Christian life is not adopting a set of rules but in discovering a personal identity in Christ?

Personal Application

Are you bound by your past or attracted by your future? For followers of Christ it's a matter of outlook. Like Lot's wife we can look back on the sensual attraction of Sodom and Gomorrah and fossilise in their ruination, or, like Abraham, we can look forward to 'the city with foundations, whose architect and builder is God' (Heb. 11:10). Where we set our eyes is where we set our hearts.

Our perspective determines our behaviour. The NIV is misleading to head this section 'Rules for Holy Living'. Paul isn't laying another set of laws on us; he is appealing for us to be who we are and urging us not slip back into who we were. Feeling good about our identity and destiny is the key to behaving well. Why crawl through the moral sewers when you are a member of the royal household of the King of kings?

Seeing Jesus in the Scriptures

Christ is at the right hand of God – the place of favour and authority. In Revelation 5, the apostle John has a remarkable insight into heaven where he sees a slain lamb revived and standing in the centre of the throne of God. The Lamb takes a sealed scroll from the right hand of the Father and in doing so takes charge of world history. Heaven's response is one of joyous, rapturous and very noisy acclamation.

When we are tempted to be earthbound in our thinking, let us focus our minds on this spiritual reality. Jesus reigns; heaven knows it, and so should we!

WEEK SIX

Spiritual Conduct

Opening Icebreaker

If you met a Christian for the first time, what kind of behaviour would you expect towards yourself and to those around you?

Bible Readings

- Colossians 3:17–4:6
- Philippians 2:12–16

Key Verse: 'And whatever you do, whether in word or deed, do it all in the name of the Lord Jesus, giving thanks to God the Father through him.' (3:17)

Focus: Personal relationships are the proving ground for authentic faith.

Opening Our Eyes

We live in an increasingly self-absorbed society. Technology allows us to commute through life with almost no awareness of our fellow travellers. We have almost limitless private entertainment literally at our fingertips, an audio-visual cornucopia that negates the need for real-world awareness and renders redundant the effort of authentic conversation. Our thrills are vicarious, our experiences private, our concerns detached.

This pathological individualism affects out spiritual lives. Many today consider their faith or spirituality to be a strictly private affair. Yet, true followers of the Way cannot do that. Faith in the Anointed profoundly affects the way that we relate to the world, especially in the need to connect with reality in our relationships. Since every act, every word, is done in Jesus' name, even the most mundane activities are to be conscious acts of shareable thanksgiving. The reality of our faith isn't measured by claims to esoteric mystical experience but by how we relate to others in God's world.

The family home is the starting place. Wives are called to joint venture in life with their husbands rather than to go it alone. Husbands are to channel their aggressive instincts and build a loving relational context for the shared adventure of life. Children should please God by respect and obedience for their parents – and fathers especially must not make demands on their children that could cause bitterness and disillusionment.

Slaves – and many are literally that in today's world, while most of us who are free nonetheless work under the orders of others – should outwork their reverence for the Lord by doing their job properly, even when no one is watching. Doing all our work for our heavenly Boss demonstrates our spiritual integrity. This is not a mental trick to make a bad job bearable; we really are Christ's servants and there are legitimate rewards for faithful employees. Likewise, there are demerits for those who serve Christ badly. Fair's fair, after all, and this Boss sees everything!

Speaking of which, if we employ others – and that includes when we hire tradesmen – we have more than a mere legal responsibility to treat them properly. We are to employ them the way that Christ employs us. That implies fair treatment and concern for them as whole people. Jesus reminds us that the measure we use for others is the same one that will be used for us – Luke 6:38.

This lifestyle in the community is to be one of passionate prayer. It has three elements: one of vigilance in the face of evil, and another of thanksgiving for the blessings of God. The third element rises from our belief that the mystery of Christ is the hope for the human race. So we are to pray for the gospel messengers, especially those suffering persecution for the sake of the message.

This gospel awareness means that we too have a testimony to bear. How we handle those who are not yet believers profoundly affects whether or not they will ever become followers of Christ. We may have spiritual insight into the mystery of Christ, but how we share that with others requires more than zeal; it needs wisdom also. In particular, our speech should be characterised by grace rather than argumentativeness or unthinking dogmatism and evangelistic aggressiveness. At the same time, it is not to be blandly pious. Godly speech is seasoned with salt that will purify and stimulate the spiritual appetite in our listeners.

Discussion Starters

1. Many people are put off the faith by the behaviour of Christians. What do you think you can do to safeguard this from happening as a result of your conduct?

_____

_____

_____

_____

2. We are a nation of moaners. What tips can you think of that will prevent us from being dragged down into the complaining culture and will enable us to be thankful people?

_____

_____

_____

_____

3. What do you consider to be the limits of obedience when you are working for someone else as a believer?

_____

_____

_____

_____

4. The notion of wifely submission has been grossly abused and we are all apt to react to it. What do you consider it really means and what sort of character must a believing husband have to make it possible?

_____

_____

_____

_____

5. What do you think is likely to embitter the children of Christian parents more than anything else?

_____

_____

_____

_____

6. Many people speak disparagingly about working for a Christian employer and stories of poor pay, worker exploitation, lack of encouragement and bad management abound. Why do you think this is and what can be done to remedy the situation?

_____

_____

_____

_____

7. The idea of rewards in heaven can be treated cynically – do-gooders lining their own nests, and all that. What constitutes a legitimate expectation of heavenly rewards?

_____

_____

_____

_____

Personal Application

Grace never forces people. It invites them. We should not command submission. Respect is earned. We have responsibilities as well as rights. People are not obliged to listen to us. Possessing the truth gives us no right to impose our beliefs on others. Nor does it excuse us from the responsibility to treat our loved ones, our work colleagues and strangers with respect. The gospel appeal must come from appealing people. Would you want to become a follower of Christ if you were viewing a DVD of your own life and speech for a week?

Seeing Jesus in the Scriptures

Jesus spent the first 30 years of His life as a dutiful son and member of a family. Many of those years were occupied in apprenticeship to His adoptive father, Joseph. In due time, He became the family breadwinner, working as a builder, fulfilling the wishes of His customers.

None of this was unspiritual or mere preparation for the 'real' work later. He was the Son of God with a hammer and chisel in His hand; the eternal Word handing over His pay packet to His mum. There is no sacred life separate from the secular. So, when the next phase of His ministry was about to begin, His heavenly Father summed up the first 30 years of His life by declaring with pride and affirmation, 'You are my Son, whom I love; with you I am well pleased' (Luke 3:22). Will He be able to say the same about us as He reviews our family, work and community lifestyle?

WEEK SEVEN

Friends in the Faith

Opening Icebreaker

Play 'A Pat on the Back'. Each member writes on the back of each person something they like about them and then others read it out for the person to hear.

Bible Readings

- Colossians 4:7–18
- John 15:9–17
- Philemon

Key Verse: 'Epaphras... servant of Christ Jesus, sends greetings. He is always wrestling in prayer for you, that you may stand firm in all the will of God, mature and fully assured.' (4:12)

Focus: The blessings of quality fellowship in the gospel.

Opening Our Eyes

The popular image of the apostle Paul is that of a fanatical, woman-hating loner. Nothing could be further from the truth. Paul headed a team of men and women whom he dearly loved and appreciated. Virtually all his letters make reference to these people and in this one he mentions a number of fellow-labourers in the gospel. They are an interesting bunch.

Tychicus was an apostolic delegate and the bearer of Paul's letters both to the Colossians and to the Ephesians. On this occasion he is accompanied by Onesimus, a slave who ran away from his Christian master, Philemon. Onesimus reached Rome and became a believer himself. Runaway slaves were liable to be tortured to death if recaptured. However, Paul sends Onesimus back to Philemon with Tychicus, together with a letter urging Philemon to receive his slave 'as a dear brother' and to treat him as if he were the apostle himself.

The Macedonian, Aristarchus, had faced public uproar in Ephesus and now shared a prison cell with Paul for the sake of the gospel. Mark (also known as John Mark) was related to Barnabas. Mark's mother, Mary, was his aunt – a woman in whose substantial house the Early Church gathered. Barnabas was one of the first to trust the reality of Paul's conversion and to grant acceptance to this former persecutor. Mark had a mixed passage. He ventured on an apostolic journey with Paul and Barnabas, travelling as far as Pamphylia but then left them, losing Paul's confidence for a time. Yet Mark went on to write the Gospel that bears his name and later was fully restored to Paul's favour.

Apart from these, Jesus Justus was the only other Jew who worked with Paul at this time. The apostle longed for the conversion of his own people and he particularly appreciated the encouragement of his fellow countrymen who did believe. Many of his trials resulted from opposition by the Jewish hierarchy, and by those who sought to hijack the message of grace by insisting it be accompanied by circumcision and ritual law.

Epaphras also did a stint in jail for his faith and is evidently a prayer warrior, interceding for the spiritual growth and well-being of the church in Colossae as well as in Laodicea and Hierapolis.

Doctor Luke is Paul's long-time companion and journal keeper and is the man who wrote the Gospel that bears his name. Demas at this point walked with God but later was to abandon his faith in favour of the attractions of this present world (2 Tim. 4:10).

Paul also greets Nympha who hosted the church in Laodicea. Although Paul, as was the case with Colossae, had not visited Laodicea in person, he clearly knew of the work and wrote a letter to the church there. This letter is now lost. Paul asks that both letters be read to both churches.

Finally, Paul has a word of prophecy for Archippus, who was a leader in the church that met in Philemon's house. It is an encouragement to fulfil the ministry to which God had called him. Paul's testimony, and that of his companions, was never triumphalist. Preaching the gospel is hard work. Opposition is normal rather than exceptional. Personal discouragement is inevitable. So, as the apostle signs off with this word of exhortation to a fellow soldier he asks, with simple grace, that they remain aware that he is in chains for the sake of the gospel.

Discussion Starters

1. Our faith is a corporate affair. There should be no lone rangers in the Church. To what extent does your group consider itself a team? How might this become more of a reality?

2. People let us down. Sometimes they bottle out of responsibility. What steps do we need to take to regain confidence in those who have failed through weakness?

3. There are many in prison for their faith and they are often neglected by human rights organisations who are more interested in political prisoners. How can we raise the profile of prisoners of faith and how can we pray effectively for them?

4. In what ways do you think we can engage practically in the fight against economic slavery?

5. One of the tests of true faith is how well we receive strangers. How well do you rate yourselves in showing hospitality to the alien, especially if they are poor and needy?

_____

_____

_____

_____

6. The House Church movement is now history, but many are discovering the value of small groups meeting in homes and other informal settings. What thoughts do you have on the future of the Church in the home?

_____

_____

_____

_____

7. Barnabas means 'Son of Encouragement'. Why not share some words of encouragement with each other to end this series of studies.

_____

_____

_____

_____

Personal Application

Black slavery may have been abolished in the West because of the work of Quakers like Thomas Clarkson and Granville Sharp (later assisted by William Wilberforce) but there is more economic slavery in the world than ever before. Once again a Christian voice needs to be raised.

The gospel transforms our personal relationships. In Christ, our status is equal irrespective of ethnicity, gender or class. Many of those in economic slavery to the West are our brothers and sisters. Paul's appeal to Philemon forbids us to ignore their plight. Although the issues are complex, we must engage politically and personally to ensure that 'third world' no longer means 'third class'.

We also have a responsibility to receive our brothers and sisters in Christ who are asylum seekers and to help them become established in our society, rather than let them become victims of exploitation.

Seeing Jesus in the Scriptures

Jesus might have proclaimed the message of the kingdom single-handedly. After all, the disciples at times seemed more trouble than they were worth! Being in such close fellowship with His Father He might have had no need for friends. Yet He chose to have companions and, in John, a very close friend – the only one who stayed with Him to the end of His life.

Jesus loved His disciples. They were never just the workforce to be organised or the captive audience for His sermons. Paul continued that pattern established by the Lord and so must we. Church should be a place of loving fellowship, not simply a gathering point for fellow activists.

Leader's Notes

Icebreaker
The Opening Icebreaker is to remind us that becoming a follower of Christ involves both leaving behind our old life and embracing the new. Repentance is more than simply being sorry; it includes embracing a Christlike life of love and kindness towards others. All you need for this icebreaker is a bowl of warm, scented water and a towel.

Aim of the Session
Throughout this series of studies get your group members to do the Bible readings. Encourage everybody to read the Introduction so that they understand what Colossians is about and why they are studying it.

Colossians is the most Christ-centred of the epistles and is incredibly relevant for today. With the growing religious pluralism in the West many want Christianity absorbed into a global pick 'n' mix religion. This is called 'syncretism'. In the face of this emerging heresy, Paul wrote to the Colossians to demonstrate that salvation is in Christ alone.

It is tempting to feel that our faith is inadequate when people point out the failures of Christianity and the successes of alternative spiritualities. It can also put us on the defensive against genuine spiritual seekers who, while despairing of historic Christianity, are open to explore our faith.

Paul's approach to such is not antagonistic; instead, he uses much of their language to lead them on a journey towards Christ. As you conduct these sessions, bear in mind the many who 'believe but do not belong', and those dissatisfied with consumerism who want something better. Our task is to guide them on their journey towards Christ. The first discussion starter invites us to examine our attitudes towards New Age seekers. Encourage people to be winsome rather than paranoid! Discussion starters 2 and 3 will help us explore the meaning of spiritual wisdom.

The first Christians called themselves 'followers of the Way'. We shall use that term to distinguish authentic faith from mere folk Christianity. An apostolic delegate named Epaphras founded the Colossian church. He joined Paul and Timothy during Paul's first Roman imprisonment and reported on the excellent lifestyle of faith, hope and love that characterised these new disciples. He also advised Paul of the spiritual challenge that threatened their young faith. This stimulated Paul to send a letter encouraging the believers. They belonged to a global movement of people discovering genuine spiritual wisdom in Christ. This comes, not through sombre religion or flesh-denying asceticism, but through a faith that fills us with joy and thanksgiving.

It also qualifies us for a glorious future. Many spiritual seekers see the body as a prison house of the soul and, by religious means, seek liberation. They want a death/rebirth experience that will grant them eternal life. This is the free gift of God to those who forsake not the body, but the sinful nature. The body is not evil; corruption is spiritual and moral. Jesus paid the price for our redemption by sacrificing His own life on our behalf.

Ask the members of your group if they know that their sins are forgiven. During His crucifixion, Jesus disarmed all coercive spiritual powers, so we can abandon the darkness of sin and death and enter His realm of light. The proof of this transformation is not renewed religious activity but transformed behaviour.

Finally, Christianity is full of jargon. Use discussion starters 5 and 6 to help folk interpret their faith for the sake of others. Paul was motivated by the heartbeat of Christ. End this session by exploring what kind of missionary vision we have and how we can make it more effective.

Week Two: Firstborn Glory

Icebreaker
The point of this icebreaker is to help people identify with Jesus as the agent of creation. As people made in His image, we too get satisfaction from making things.

Aim of the Session
You will need to explain what an 'icon' is. Some may think of an icon as no more than religious superstition; others will think of computer icons. Spiritually speaking, an 'icon' is a representation of reality and a doorway to reality. Jesus is the icon of the Father. The term 'Father' may be understood as Divine Source, for He is the eternal source of the Son. When Jesus is described as the 'firstborn' of creation, the term represents seniority rather than point of origin. It means He is the rightful Heir of the universe, rather than the first one made. When Jesus walked the earth, He spent 30 years as a construction engineer, but before the dawn of time as the eternal Son, He had put together the entire cosmos. Scientists search for the fundamental forces that hold the universe together, but revelation tells us that the Son is the divine glue.

How do we know what God is really like, since nobody can see Him? The Son reveals God as He really is and we must interpret our entire understanding of God through the human–divine Jesus. We discover that God is vulnerable; His love is sacrificial and will pay the ultimate price for our reconciliation. Explore with members of your group just how they view God. Many so stress His sovereignty that they neglect His vulnerable desire to win us to Himself.

Nature models a cycle of death and resurrection that points to the death and physical resurrection of Christ and the promise of a new creation. Jesus is the first of that new creation in time and in seniority, just as He was of the first creation. We now have a Man in charge of the universe. He is invested with the full essence of God and commissioned to bring about the reconciliation of all that is disordered, damaged and corrupted. This is one of the most mind-blowing truths in the Bible. Allow members of the group to explore the far-reaching dimensions of this truth.

God might have started this reconciliation with a new breed of people; Jesus could have married and had children, but He did not. He began by inviting His enemies to be reconciled and to join a stream of renewed humanity. These people form the Church of which He is the Head. All we need is simple faith. Lengthy self-help programmes will never save us. By faith in Him, we can join this new creation and play our part in His ministry of reconciliation.

Church often receives a bad press and sometimes deservedly so. We need to return to an understanding of the Church as the Body of Christ, made up of people whose lives demonstrate steadfastness and love. Let others mock but we will continue to demonstrate God's grace in 'clay pots' and, by His Spirit's power, tell every single person in the world about God's wonderful offer of reconciliation.

Use the discussion starters to talk about the superiority of the Son. We can have utter confidence in Him. Faith in Jesus is neither second-hand, second-rate, nor redundant. With so many people seeking spiritual techniques and experiences, we should have confidence in the Way and promote Him without fear or shame.

Finally, use discussion starter 7 to explore practical ways that we can help one another remain faithful through the trials and tests of life.

Week Three: The Mystery Uncovered

Icebreaker

'Pass-the-Parcel' is a well-known and easy game. The point of doing it in this session is to remind us that there is a mystery about the Christian faith and it is one that is progressively revealed during our spiritual journey. Wrap a hard boiled egg in cotton wool, then wrap it round with many layers of paper, string and Sellotape.

Aim of the Session

The Roman Empire had many mystery religions that offered enlightenment through progressive degrees of spiritual initiation. The offers remain, but the real mystery and the point of the true spiritual journey is Christ. Sadly, many have viewed and even shared in the outward forms of Christianity without ever discovering the mystery. It leaves them with no more than a religious lifestyle that is understandably despised by many spiritual seekers today.

The term 'Christ' relates to the Old Testament Messiah and at its heart is the notion of a King anointed with the Spirit of God. Jesus is the Man more filled with the Holy Spirit than any other. He is also the King of kings and Lord of lords. Explain that the Jewish people often saw this nationalistically and so struggled with Jesus of Nazareth. Gentiles, of course, knew nothing of this at all.

Paul was one of many Jews who encountered Christ. The revelation of this mystery astounded and captivated him. He had discovered that we could be 'enchristed'. Human beings are not simply electrochemical machines. We are spirit-dependant creatures, always possessed and serving some spirit or other. A religion that offers no spiritual experience leaves us unchanged and unsatisfied. Authentic faith in Jesus means letting ourselves be invaded by the Spirit of Christ. It makes all the difference. His personal presence is the essence of spiritual life and also guarantees a glorious future. This is not the doctrinal preserve of charismatics or Pentecostals, but the secret discovery of all who are sufficiently honest, dedicated and humble enough to find it. Explore with members of the group how far they have travelled along this road.

If this transcendent experience of Christ in us by His Spirit is so important, surely we should want everyone to enter its mysterious depths? Paul was prepared to share in the ongoing sufferings of Christ to bring this news to the whole world. How passionate are we to do likewise? We have crossed the threshold to the meaning of life. It is all found in exploring Christ, and we should invite everyone to join us in the quest.

Remind people that apostolic tradition is more than doctrine; it is life-consuming passion. Seek to lead your group to rekindle that passion and enable them no longer to take for granted what it means to have Christ in us.

Use discussion starter 4 to explore Paul's claim to make up what is lacking in Christ's afflictions. Jesus did everything necessary to secure our salvation, but He continues in travail to bring that salvation to birth in the lives of men and women through the proclamation of the gospel. He bears those sufferings in the sufferings of His people as they seek to spread the message. His pain is our pain; our pain is His pain.

Use discussion starters 1 and 2 to talk about being filled with the Spirit. There is only one Anointed, so being filled with the Spirit is not a private, independent experience; we share together in the anointing of Christ. Some members of the group may wish to be prayed for at this time.

The Church of Christ continues to suffer around the world. Discuss how we can assist our persecuted brothers and sisters, and how we might find the courage to share our faith in the face of opposition.

Week Four: True and False Spirituality

Icebreaker
In this fun exercise, try to avoid simply reinventing Christianity! The point is to differentiate between religion and authentic faith. Include features such as rituals, initiation rites, and rules.

Aim of the Session
Most people are irritated and angry about religion, especially the fundamentalist kind. Who can blame them? Others describe themselves as 'spiritual', but not 'religious'. Yet the secular world is not neutral. Western humanism is a fundamentalist religion driven, like all religions, by the 'basic principles of this world' – 'the lust of the flesh, the lust of the eyes, and the pride of life'.

Religion does not compare with the Anointed Son. Our faith may seem unsophisticated, but Christ is risen from the dead and contains all the virtues and eternal essence of God Himself. He is the supreme authority over all other authorities. Everyone who follows Him gets to share His fullness of spiritual life. We have every reason to be proud of Jesus.

Most philosophies and religions have a form of rebirthing: an initiatory ritual, confession or dedicatory act. Entering spiritual union and identification with Christ is sometimes tritely called being 'born again', like a makeover, but it is the genuinely spiritual experience that alone gives meaning to ritual representations like baptism. Regeneration truly frees us from slavery of sin and the sinful nature and grants us spiritual life.

Jesus lived this out on our behalf. He willingly entered our slavery to liberate us. On the cross, He took our contract of slavery – all the rules and regulations imposed by our culture, religion, ancestry – and crucified it. In a triumph of grace, He publicly disempowered our former slave owners. Encourage your group members to explore the depths of this truth.

We are complete in Christ, so don't return to the shadowlands of religious legalism, be it formal religion, political creed or secular cultural conformity. Why take up with some New Age novelty when you have everything in Christ? Why be impressed by people claiming unique visions and supposed spiritual insights? Who needs gurus when you have access to the Master Himself?

Techno-minded people love making up rules that are supposed to better us. They tell us what to eat, what to wear, what meditation techniques to use – we are up to our eyes in self-help programmes – but none of them can give us eternal life. Dismantle some of the supposed remedies for our ills and expose them for what they are – just another form of vanity.

Given that the answers lie fully in Jesus, why isn't everyone flocking to church? Sadly, so much of church fails to demonstrate this fullness of spiritual life. Christians can be more hidebound and rigid than non-Christians. Inner peace and grace often seem lacking and, worse, when we buy into novel self-help technologies we demonstrate our failure to find the answers in Jesus. We must accept the challenge of true union with Christ. Encourage your group to seek nothing less and to avoid being captivated by 'the basic principles of this world'.

During the discussion time, explore why people are seeking alternative spiritual answers to their lives. What do we have to offer? Discussion starter 2 provides us with the opportunity to give real meaning to the term 'born again'. Use discussion starters 3, 4, 6 and 7 to talk about destructive legalism in our lives and how union with Christ abolishes its need.

Discussion starter 5 allows us to discuss how other religions, secular humanism and political philosophies fail to give real answers to the human condition. Don't let this become party political, instead keep centred on Christ.

Week Five: Old Man, New Man

Icebreaker
The Opening Icebreaker may be a reality for immigrant members of your group, but let's imagine if all of us had emigrated. Becoming a believer is not a matter of joining the Church, and retaining our former lifestyle and identity. We must embrace fully what it means to be a citizen of heaven.

Aim of the Session
There are only two kinds of people in this world – those who are in Adam and those who are in Christ. Those in Adam are spiritually dead and will not inherit eternal life. Those in Christ have experienced a spiritual rebirth and will share the eternal glory of Jesus. It is only possible to move from one to the other by going through a death and rebirth experience that requires us to leave behind our Adam-citizenship and embrace our Christ-citizenship.

If this has happened, then our life is encrypted in God and Christ is the unbreakable algorithm. In other words, no one can steal your spiritual life and inheritance. This security gives us grounds to live for the future and frees us from our bondage to the past. We can reject the typical attitudes of Adam's race because we have undergone an inner identity change. The old self has gone and now we are beginning to learn what it is like to be a new creature in Christ Jesus. He now defines who we are, and what we want to be. This means we will wish to embrace the virtues of Christ. Take the opportunity to contrast the attitudes of Adam with the attitudes of Christ. It is time for us to be true to ourselves in Him.

This really is not a matter of taking on a new set of rules. Instead, it is more to do with a genuine self-perception and of learning how to behave in accordance with who we are becoming, rather than who we have been. Many followers of Jesus have a very inadequate appreciation of this truth and this is a major reason why the Christian life seems so difficult for them.

Our future destiny is to be with Jesus. He is already at the right hand of the Father and is in charge of world history. The more we have our eyes focused on Him and on our ultimate destiny, the easier it is to live like Him. Use discussion starter 1 to imagine what the future will be like. Don't get bogged down in theories about the second coming of Christ, but do anticipate it with great joy.

Use discussion starters 2, 3 and 4 to stress how the proof of true spirituality is demonstrated by the quality of our behaviour towards others. Claiming great spiritual experiences is no substitute for loving our neighbours.

Discussion starter 5 should remind us that worship is much more than the Sunday set piece in the special building. It is a way of life. We are to give thanks in every situation. Holy ground is wherever we place our feet. Concerning acts of worship, we should not let our musical, liturgical, or other preferences dictate our willingness to worship. Nor should we consider that biblical instruction is confined to sermons and Bible studies such as this. Explore how we can encourage one another in a worshipful lifestyle and how we can helpfully bring the truth of God to bear on each other's lifestyles.

The final discussion starter invites us to challenge the common belief that Christians are simply people obeying badly a set of self-imposed rules. How can we communicate the reality of a new identity in Christ to a poorly instructed world?

Week Six: Spiritual Conduct

Icebreaker
This icebreaker asks us to imagine that we are not followers of Christ. What would we expect of those who are? Be careful, because that's what non-Christians expect of you!

Aim of the Session
Self-absorption is an increasing and sad characteristic of our society. It is made all the worse if we have inherited the individualism of an island race. There should be little room for 'me and Jesus' in our lives – it is 'us and Him'. That is why we pray 'Our Father' and not 'My Father'. True spirituality is communal. It touches all our relationships and engages us in society. Rather than withdrawing from the world, we seek to engage the world with the transforming power of Christ within us. There can be no sacred and secular divide. The life of Christ affects every single moment, every activity, every word, thought and deed, every encounter with others.

This begins in the family home. Creation birthed the fundamental relationship between husband and wife. This is often an abused one and it has led to the breakdown of so much in our society. Marriage is a calling – a calling for wives to 'joint venture' with their husbands. Submission is not to be commanded by a husband. It is a free choice to join a man in the adventure of life, rather than to go solo. Husbands are called to do something useful with their instinctive aggression and to build a protective, relational context for their wives. Discuss the reality of what this means by using discussion starter 4.

Children honour God by doing as they are told, but fathers must not lay cruel burdens on their children. The cruellest and commonest is desertion, but being insensitive to children's needs, having one standard for them and another for ourselves, is deeply harmful.

Paul takes the extreme example of slavery to talk about the outworking of faith in the workplace. Slaves had no rights whatsoever; they were often treated appallingly and felt they owed nothing to their masters. Since Christians are willing slaves of Christ, whatever our employment situation – and most of us are not actually slaves – we should serve our bosses by serving our real Boss.

It was a radical thought to suggest that slave owners should treat slaves as human beings. It led many Christian slave-owners in the Early Church to liberate their slaves. Use discussion starter 6 to discuss why so many Christian employers have a reputation for bad employment of their staff. What has gone wrong and how can we do better than the world?

Prayer is a way of life for the truly spiritual and all prayer revolves around Christ being the hope for the human race.

Instead of criticising the proclaimers of the faith we should be praying for them, particularly those who suffer. Yet in praying for others, we must remember that we are all called to be ambassadors for Christ in our own context. This is a call for wisdom as well as zeal. Insensitive evangelisation will do more harm than good. Our speech should be provocative, but it should also be full of grace. Encourage the members of your group to discuss what this means in practice.

Most of us will witness for Christ in our own country, among our own people and in the ordinariness of life. Jesus spent most of His life like this. Remind folk that our missionary call begins every day when we get out of bed.

Week Seven: Friends in the Faith

Icebreaker
To play this game, make 'Post-it' notes available. People will object to someone writing on their clothes! The idea is to write something appreciative and stick these notes on one another and then get others to read to the person what has been written about them.

Aim of the Session
The life and teaching of Paul has thrilled and angered people for centuries. Today, many parody him as a religious nutcase who hated women. This common view is utterly false. Paul was a team player who loved and appreciated both the men and the women who served Christ alongside him. This letter mentions a number of them.

Onesimus was a runaway slave who arrived in Rome and became a believer. His master, Philemon, had also become a follower of Christ. While writing to the Colossians, Paul pens a letter to Philemon urging him to receive Onesimus as a brother. He commissions Tychicus to accompany Onesimus, probably to help the latter avoid the slave catchers. A runaway slave could be tortured to death. By insisting that he be treated as a brother, Paul undermined the entire concept of slavery. With so much slavery in the world today, use discussion starter 4 to explore how we can end it.

Paul's companions were typical of the network of relationships in the Early Church. Barnabas had befriended Paul at his conversion. His aunt, Mary, housed the Early Church. She was also Mark's mother. Mark lost Paul's favour, leading to a separation between Paul and Barnabas. Yet it was Mark who wrote the Gospel, and later on, Paul welcomed him back.

Most of Paul's companions were Gentiles, yet some, like Jesus Justus, were fellow countrymen, reminding us that Paul longed for the conversion of the Jews – as should we.

Aristarchus and Epaphras were with Paul in prison. That didn't stop Epaphras from continuing his prayer ministry for the churches in Colossae, Laodicea and Hierapolis. Remind folk that those in constrained circumstances can still minister powerfully before the Lord.

Luke, the doctor and long-term companion of Paul's, kept the diary that later became the book of Acts. He also wrote the Gospel. Tragically, Demas later abandoned the faith in favour of the pleasures of life.

Paul had visited neither Colossae nor Laodicea, but he knew of the Church that met in the house of Nympha. He asked that this letter be read to the Church in Laodicea, also. Archippus was a leading figure in the Church that met in Philemon's house and Paul encourages him to keep going in his faith and ministry.

We sense the affection and esteem with which Paul held his fellow workers. Those who serve Christ can only do so effectively if they have formed deep relationships of love and trust. Use the discussion starters 1 and 7 to talk about how we can improve our relationships.

The home plays an important part in the life of God's people. Hospitality is a virtue. Without endorsing any one form of church, how can we effectively use our homes to win others to the faith? Discussion starters 5 and 6 remind us of our biblical responsibility towards asylum seekers and others who become our neighbours.

We have a particular responsibility to pray and work for the release of prisoners of faith who are often ignored by a bigoted media. Use discussion starter 3 to find ways that we can help our brothers and sisters.

This letter ends with the personal signature of Paul and the plaintive request that they think about him in his own imprisonment for the sake of a salvation that is found in Christ alone.

Notes...

Notes...

Notes...

Notes...

The *Cover to Cover* Bible Study Series

James
Faith in action
ISBN: 978-1-85345-293-2

Jeremiah
The passionate prophet
ISBN: 978-1-85345-372-4

Job
The source of wisdom
ISBN: 978-1-78259-992-0

Joel
Getting real with God
ISBN: 978-1-78951-927-2

John's Gospel
Exploring the seven miraculous signs
ISBN: 978-1-85345-295-6

Jonah
Rescued from the depths
ISBN: 978-1-78259-762-9

Joseph
The power of forgiveness and reconciliation
ISBN: 978-1-85345-252-9

Joshua 1-10
Hand in hand with God
ISBN: 978-1-85345-542-7

Joshua 11-24
Called to service
ISBN: 978-1-78951-138-3

Judges 1-8
The spiral of faith
ISBN: 978-1-85345-681-7

Judges 9-21
Learning to live God's way
ISBN: 978-1-85345-910-8

Luke
A prescription for living
ISBN: 978-1-78259-270-9

Mark
Life as it is meant to be lived
ISBN: 978-1-85345-233-8

Mary
The mother of Jesus
ISBN: 978-1-78259-402-4

Moses
Face to face with God
ISBN: 978-1-85345-336-6

Names of God
Exploring the depths of God's character
ISBN: 978-1-85345-680-0

Nehemiah
Principles for life
ISBN: 978-1-85345-335-9

Parables
Communicating God on earth
ISBN: 978-1-85345-340-3

Philemon
From slavery to freedom
ISBN: 978-1-85345-453-0

Philippians
Living for the sake of the gospel
ISBN: 978-1-85345-421-9

Prayers of Jesus
Hearing His heartbeat
ISBN: 978-1-85345-647-3

Proverbs
Living a life of wisdom
ISBN: 978-1-85345-373-1

Psalms
Songs of life
ISBN: 978-1-78951-240-3

Revelation 1-3
Christ's call to the Church
ISBN: 978-1-85345-461-5

Revelation 4-22
The Lamb wins! Christ's final victory
ISBN: 978-1-85345-411-0

Rivers of Justice
Responding to God's call to righteousness today
ISBN: 978-1-85345-339-7

Ruth
Loving kindness in action
ISBN: 978-1-85345-231-4

Song of Songs
A celebration of love
ISBN: 978-1-78259-959-3

The Armour of God
Living in His strength
ISBN: 978-1-78259-583-0

The Beatitudes
Immersed in the grace of Christ
ISBN: 978-1-78259-495-6

The Creed
Belief in action
ISBN: 978-1-78259-202-0

The Divine Blueprint
God's extraordinary power in ordinary lives
ISBN: 978-1-85345-292-5

The Holy Spirit
Understanding and experiencing Him
ISBN: 978-1-85345-254-3

The Image of God
His attributes and character
ISBN: 978-1-85345-228-4

The Kingdom
Studies from Matthew's Gospel
ISBN: 978-1-85345-251-2

The Letter to the Colossians
In Christ alone
ISBN: 978-1-855345-405-9

The Letter to the Romans
Good news for everyone
ISBN: 978-1-85345-250-5

The Lord's Prayer
Praying Jesus' way
ISBN: 978-1-85345-460-8

The Prodigal Son
Amazing grace
ISBN: 978-1-85345-412-7

The Second Coming
Living in the light of Jesus' return
ISBN: 978-1-85345-422-6

The Sermon on the Mount
Life within the new covenant
ISBN: 978-1-85345-370-0

Thessalonians
Building Church in changing times
ISBN: 978-1-78259-443-7

The Ten Commandments
Living God's Way
ISBN: 978-1-85345-593-3

The Uniqueness of our Faith
What makes Christianity distinctive?
ISBN: 978-1-85345-232-1

For current prices or to order, visit **cwr.org.uk/shop**
Available online or from Christian bookshops.

Be inspired by God.
Every day.

Confidently face life's challenges by equipping yourself daily with God's Word. There is something for everyone...

Every Day with Jesus

Selwyn Hughes' renowned writing is updated by Mick Brooks into these trusted and popular notes.

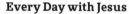

Inspiring Women
Every Day

Encouragement, uplifting scriptures and insightful daily thoughts for women.

Life Every Day

Jeff Lucas helps apply the Bible to daily life with his trademark humour and insight.

The Manual

Straight-talking guides to help men walk daily with God. Written by Carl Beech.

To find out more about all our daily Bible reading notes, or to take out a subscription, visit **cwr.org.uk/biblenotes** or call 01252 784700.
Also available in Christian bookshops.

 Printed format   Large print format   Email format   Ebook format

SmallGroup central

All of our small group ideas and resources in one place

Online:

smallgroupcentral.org.uk
is filled with free video teaching, tools, articles and a whole host of ideas.

On the road:

A range of seminars themed for small groups can be brought to your local community. Contact us at **hello@smallgroupcentral.org.uk**

In print:

Books, study guides and DVDs covering an extensive list of themes, Bible books and life issues.

Find out more at:
smallgroupcentral.org.uk

Courses and events

Waverley Abbey College

Publishing and media

Conference facilities

Transforming lives

CWR's vision is to enable people to experience personal transformation through applying God's Word to their lives and relationships.

Our Bible-based training and resources help people around the world to:
• Grow in their walk with God
• Understand and apply Scripture to their lives
• Resource themselves and their church
• Develop pastoral care and counselling skills
• Train for leadership
• Strengthen relationships, marriage and family life and much more.

CWR Applying God's Word
to everyday life and relationships

CWR, Waverley Abbey House,
Waverley Lane, Farnham,
Surrey GU9 8EP, UK

Telephone: **+44 (0)1252 784700**
Email: **info@cwr.org.uk**
Website: **cwr.org.uk**

Registered Charity No. 294387
Company Registration No. 1990308

Our insightful writers provide daily Bible reading notes and other resources for all ages, and our experienced course designers and presenters have gained an international reputation for excellence and effectiveness.

CWR's Training and Conference Centre in Surrey, England, provides excellent facilities in an idyllic setting – ideal for both learning and spiritual refreshment.